It's CHRISTMAS!

ALL ABOUT
CHRISTMAS ANGELS

KRISTEN RAJCZAK NELSON

PowerKiDS press™

NEW YORK

Published in 2020 by The Rosen Publishing Group, Inc.
29 East 21st Street, New York, NY 10010

First Edition

Editor: Kristen Rajczak Nelson
Book Design: Reann Nye

Photo Credits: Cover Harry Fodor/EyeEm/Getty Images; p. 5 Westend61/Getty Images; p. 7 https://commons.wikimedia.org/wiki/File:Bartolom%C3%A9_Esteban_Perez_Murillo_023.jpg; p. 9 Christophel Fine Art/Universal Images Group/Getty Images; p. 11 Cio/Shutterstock.com; p. 13 Gwoeii/Shutterstock.com; p. 15 © www.istockphoto.com/PoppyPixels; p. 17 3523studio/Shutterstock.com; p. 19 Hulton Archive/Getty Images; p. 21 © www.istockphoto.com/izzzy71; p. 22 Alexxndr/Shutterstock.com.

Cataloging-in-Publication Data
Names: Rajczak Nelson, Kristen.
Title: All about christmas angels / Kristen Rajczak Nelson.
Description: New York : PowerKids Press, 2020. | Series: It's Christmas! | Includes glossary and index.
Identifiers: ISBN 9781725300644 (pbk.) | ISBN 9781725300668 (library bound) | ISBN 9781725300651 (6pack)
Subjects: LCSH: Angels–Juvenile literature. | Jesus Christ–Nativity–Juvenile literature.
Classification: LCC BL477.R35 2020 | DDC 202'.15–dc23

CPSIA Compliance Information: Batch #CSPK19. For Further Information contact Rosen Publishing, New York, New York at 1-800-237-9932.

CONTENTS

CHRISTMAS ANGELS

The word "angel" comes from a Greek word that means "messenger." In the Christian **faith** and others, angels are believed to be messengers of God. So why are angels so often found on top of Christmas trees today? These messengers are a big part of the story of the first Christmas!

4

5

BIBLE STORIES

Angels are part of many stories in the Bible. This is the most important book to people who follow the Christian faith. The angel Gabriel visited a girl named Mary and told her she was going to be the mother of God's son, Jesus. It's Jesus's birth that Christians **celebrate** at Christmas.

The Bible says an angel also visited Mary's soon-to-be husband, Joseph, to tell him he would be Jesus's father on Earth. Then, when Jesus was born, angels appeared in the sky! They told **shepherds** in the fields that the son of God had been born in the town of Bethlehem.

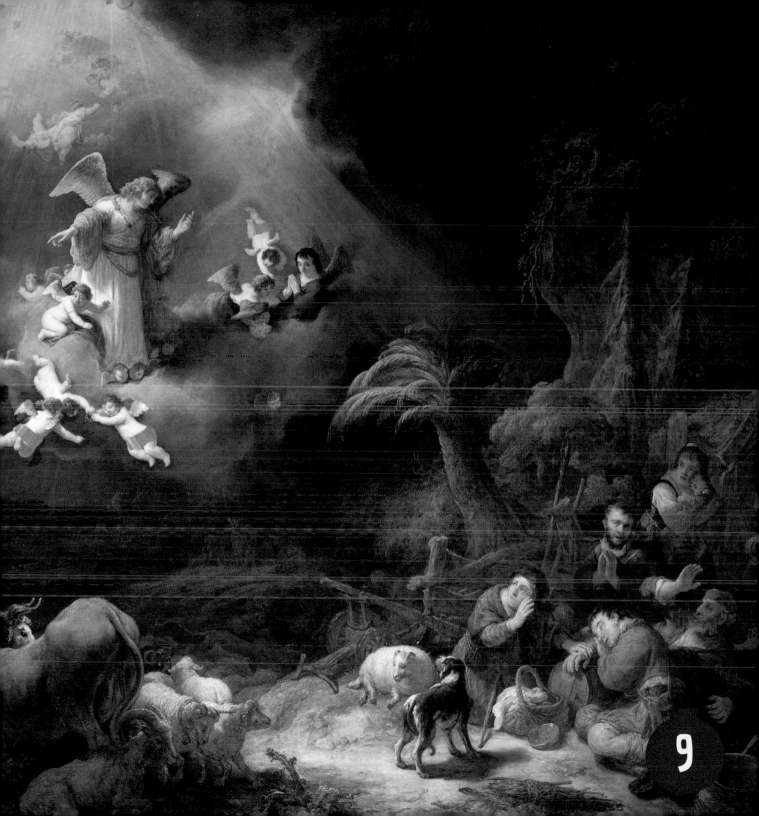

9

ON THE TREE

These Bible stories are the reason angels are a **symbol** of the Christmas season. That didn't happen right away, though! For a long time, Christians had other beliefs about angels. Some believed angels were minds without bodies. But by the 1500s, people began to place angel shapes on Christmas trees.

Angels became tree toppers because placing them higher made them more like the angels in the sky after Jesus was born. Christians believed that putting them on their trees might scare away dark spirits, too! People were beginning to think of angels as **protectors** of people on Earth.

13

Angels made another mark on Christmas trees—tinsel! These shiny streamers became part of the holiday when Christians of the past told their children that angels **decorated** their Christmas tree. The streamers on the tree were strands of hair the angels had left behind! At first, this "angel hair" was paper. It later was made of the metals silver and aluminum.

15

Angels were put on trees in other ways, too! At first, people baked angel cookies for trees or made angel **ornaments** of straw. In the 1800s, they began to make angel ornaments out of glass. Now, Christmas angels are made of all kinds of **materials** and may play music or light up!

THE QUEEN'S ANGEL

Angel tree toppers became more popular after 1848. A drawing of the queen of England's Christmas tree showed the queen's family around a tree with an angel on top. More people in Great Britain and the United States began choosing to get a tree and to place an angel at the top.

CHRISTMAS ANGELS TODAY

It's common today for people to have Christmas trees. These trees may have angels on them even if their owners aren't of the Christian faith. Christmas angels are often shown wearing white. They have wings and a **halo**. This look comes from old paintings. The angels on your tree might look a bit more playful!

20

Angels have become a symbol of light and hope for the whole year. Many people believe that a **guardian** angel watches over them! Many people who aren't part of the Christian faith also believe in angels.

Whatever you choose to believe, angels will always be a lovely part of Christmas!

22

GLOSSARY

celebrate: To do something special for a day or event.

decorate: To make something look nice by adding something to it.

faith: A set of beliefs someone follows.

guardian: Someone who watches over another.

halo: A circle of light around the head of a holy person in some art.

material: Something from which something else can be made.

ornament: A small, fancy object put on something else to make it look nice.

protector: One who keeps others safe.

shepherd: Someone who takes care of sheep.

symbol: Something that stands for something else.

INDEX

WEBSITES

Due to the changing nature of Internet links, PowerKids Press has developed an online list of websites related to the subject of this book. This site is updated regularly. Please use this link to access the list: www.powerkidslinks.com/IC/angels